P9-DNN-242

THIS CANDLEWICK BIOGRAPHY BELONGS TO:

LADY LIBERTY

Doreen Rappaport

For Mary Lee Donovan, who liberates words –D. R.
To my grandmother, Pauline Hickey, who came to America in 1936 –M. T.

Text copyright © 2008 by Doreen Rappaport. Illustrations copyright © 2008 by Matt Tavares. All rights reserved. No part of this book may be reproduced, transmitted, or stored in an information retrieval system in any form or by any means, graphic, electronic, or mechanical, including photocopying, taping, and recording, without prior written permission from the publisher. First edition in this format 2014. Library of Congress Cataloging-in-Publication Data is available. Library of Congress Catalog Card Number 2007040723. ISBN 978-0-7636-2530-6 (hardcover). ISBN 978-0-7636-5301-9 (paperback). ISBN 978-0-7636-7114-3 (reformatted hardcover). ISBN 978-0-7636-7115-0 (reformatted paperback). This book was typeset in Minion Condensed. The illustrations were done in watercolor, ink, and pencil. Candlewick Press, 99 Dover Street, Somerville, Massachusetts 02144. visit us at www.candlewick.com. Printed in Dongguan, Guangdong, China. 14 15 16 17 18 19 TLF 10 9 8 7 6 5 4 3 2 1

A BIOGRAPHY

illustrated by Matt Tavares

CANDLEWICK PRESS

· TABLE OF CONTENTS ·

DOREEN RAPPAPORT
New York City, Today

One hundred twenty years ago,
my grandfather fled his home in Latvia,
thousands of miles away.
He left his mother and father and
brothers and sisters and
aunts and uncles and cousins
to come to a country where he knew no one.
He came to build a better life.

As the ferry nears the Statue of Liberty,
I try to imagine his ocean journey and
how he felt when he saw her for the first time.

He was on a ship packed with people
from many different countries,
speaking languages he did not understand.
For days the ocean bucked and roared.
He slept in steerage with others who had no money,
longing for fresh air.
Most days his stomach hurt too much to eat.

Then early one morning, shouts of
"The Lady! The Lady!" awakened him.
He raced up to the deck.
The ship was pulling into New York,
and there was Lady Liberty greeting them all.

Arms reached out as if to caress her.
People lifted babies so they could see her.
Tears ran down my grandfather's face.
People around him were crying, too.
And then a wave of cheering and hugging
swept over the ship.

I wonder if my grandfather ever thought
about how she came to be.

ÉDOUARD DE LABOULAYE

Professor of Law
Glatigny, France, 1865

It is a warm summer night.
After dinner, we move into the parlor.
The talk turns to our dear friend, America.

We speak of how the Marquis de Lafayette
fought side by side with George Washington.
Ever the historian, Henri Martin reminds us
that the Americans would not have won
the final battle at Yorktown
without Count de Grasse's navy
and Rochambeau's soldiers.
Our countrymen died for America's freedom.

The American Revolution fired our revolution.
Their Declaration of Independence inspired our
Declaration of the Rights of Man and of the Citizen.
I often tell my own students that the
American Constitution is a model for the world.

Soon America will be one hundred years old.
I share my dream of a birthday gift.
Auguste Bartholdi listens intently when
I suggest a monument from our people to theirs
to celebrate their one hundred years of independence
and to honor one hundred years of friendship
between our countries.

Henri says such a gift is not possible now.
Emperor Napoleon III rules France.
This dictator would not allow such a gift.
I will wait for things to change, I say.
I will not give up my dream.

AUGUSTE BARTHOLDI
Sculptor
40 rue Vavin, Paris, France, 1875

Laboulaye's dream has become my dream, too.
Now after ten years of dreaming,
we can make it come true—
Napoleon III rules France no more.

I went across the sea to America to share the dream.
Laboulaye gave me letters of introduction.
I met many famous people,
including President Ulysses S. Grant.
Everyone was polite and seemed interested.
But no one offered to raise money to build her.
I am not worried.
We will raise the money in France.

Everything in America is so big.
The mighty Niagara Falls pounds liquid thunder.
Tall grasses stretch across a never-ending prairie.
Jagged peaks soar in the Rocky Mountains.
California's giant redwoods cover the sky.
In this New World of colossal natural wonders,
I found the perfect place for her.
She will rise on an island in New York's harbor,
welcoming everyone to America.

I have sketched Liberty many times
and made clay models.
Laboulaye helped me at every stage.
She will be massive but elegant,
as grand as any one of the
Seven Wonders of the Ancient World.
Liberty will rival the Great Pyramid of Egypt,
and the gold and ivory statue of Zeus at Olympia,
and the colossus of Helios in Rhodes.

MARIE SIMON
Bartholdi's Assistant
25 rue de Chazelles, Paris, France, 1876

After months of work,
we have finished the right arm and torch.
Now we start on the left hand.
We go back to Bartholdi's four-foot clay model.

The pointers measure her forearm, wrist,
fingers, nails, and tablet.
They multiply each part by two
to build a model twice as big.

Again, they measure and multiply,
this time by four.
Slowly. Carefully. Section by section,
the workers build a bigger model.
Bartholdi moves about like a prowling tiger,
reminding everyone to be precise.

Again, measure and multiply by four.
This third model pleases Bartholdi.
The workers divide it into twenty-one parts.
Each part will be enlarged another four times.

Now the carpenters begin.
Day in, day out, buzzing and sawing.
Wood chips and sawdust litter the floor.
Narrow wooden strips are bent and
nailed together to form the giant molds.
Some wood is carved to make softer lines.

White dust clings to the workers
as they pour plaster over the wood
until the shapes are just right.
Bartholdi waits impatiently
for the plaster to harden.

New wooden molds have been set on the plaster.
Now the coppersmiths begin their work.

"I will not cast her like ancient statues
from bronze cannons taken from enemies,"
Bartholdi says.
"She will be of pure copper,
made by workers in an era of peace."

Liberty's copper skin will not rust
in the salt air of the New York harbor.
Copper is light and easy to work.
It bends without cracking.

Day in, day out, rapping and banging,
as the copper is pounded on the molds
until the shapes are perfect.
Bartholdi stalks about the studio
from station to station,
hurrying the workers along,
oblivious to the noise.

Finally the hollow copper shells
are lifted off the wooden molds.
Now it is Eiffel's turn.
He must make sure Liberty stands tall.

GUSTAVE EIFFEL
Structural Engineer
25 rue de Chazelles, Paris, France, 1883

Lady Liberty is the talk of Paris.
Every day hundreds of people come
to watch her grow.

To keep Liberty upright is a challenge
as great as any I have faced in building bridges.
Her copper shell weighs more than 179,000 pounds.
So I made her a skeleton—
a ninety-six-foot-high iron tower
of beams and ribs
upon which to bolt her copper skin.

Iron rusts when it touches copper.
Some say my brilliance is having
the beams pass through fittings
so the iron does not fasten directly to the copper.
The fittings also let her copper skin move,
to expand and contract with the weather.

I listen to the people talk as they watch
her skin being riveted onto her skeleton.
She inspires them. She inspires me.
Liberté, égalité, and *fraternité* are in the air.

EMMA LAZARUS
Poet
New York City, November 1883

A gala auction is being held
to raise money for Liberty's pedestal.
Famous artists are donating paintings.
I was asked to write a poem
to be sold along with poems
by Longfellow and Whitman.
It is a great honor to be asked.
I can write about anything I want.
But I have had trouble writing lately
because I feel too sad.

In the past few years in Russia,
hundreds of Jews have been killed.
Thousands have been persecuted,
their homes burned, their shops destroyed.
They trek hundreds of miles across Europe
with only the clothes on their backs,
hoping to find ships to take them to America.

We Jews are not new to hatred.
Almost two hundred years ago
my ancestors fled Europe, too.
America was a land of hope for them.
It is still a land of hope.

Soon when people arrive in the New World,
they will be welcomed
by a caring, powerful woman.

Give me your tired, your poor,
Your huddled masses yearning to breathe free,
The wretched refuse of your teeming shore.
Send these, the homeless, tempest-tost to me:
I lift my lamp beside the golden door!

CHARLES P. STONE
Construction Supervisor
Bedloe's Island, March 1884

Sweat and grime cover the workers' bodies.
Their muscles bulge from months of digging.
They grunt and call out to one another
in words foreign to my ears
as they hack away with pickaxes
at old cisterns and stone walls,
until the hole is thirteen feet deep
and ninety-one feet square.

They mix and pour cement and sand
and large and small stones
to fill the huge hole.
They pour more concrete on top,
27,000 tons in all, until the foundation
rises sixty-five feet from the ground.
They test each layer to be sure
it is hard before they pour again.

Over and over, sixteen hours a day,
their rhythms never change,
only the weather.
Every part of their bodies aches,
but no one complains.
There were no jobs in their villages
in Italy.

When the sun goes down, they eat,
then stumble off to sleep
in makeshift tents on the island.
But I believe they are content, for
they are building new lives in this country.

JOSEPH PULITZER
Publisher, New York *World*
New York City, March 1885

More than one hundred thousand French people—
shopkeepers, artisans, farmers, and children—
gave their hard-earned money to build Liberty.
Americans have been giving money, too.
One hundred thousand dollars is still needed
to build her pedestal.
Some Americans criticize the French
for not giving all the money, since it is a gift.
I read with disgust newspaper editorials
mocking their generosity.

Some people call Liberty a "national disgrace."
Others call her "New York's lighthouse."
The mayor of New York City does not want her.
Congress has refused to give money for her pedestal.
I cannot understand why politicians do not understand
her power as a symbol of freedom.

I say she belongs in New York City.
New York is the gateway to the New World,
the door of hope for immigrants.
I know.
I landed here penniless twenty-one years ago.

We have more than a hundred millionaires in this city
who could write a check for the full amount.
But no one has.
I shall ask my readers to help.
They are not millionaires,
but I know they will care,
for they will understand her importance.

FLORENCE DE FOREEST
Metuchen, New Jersey, June 1885

Mr. Pulitzer's campaign is working.
More than one hundred thousand
Americans have given
pennies, nickels, dimes, and dollars.
When you send money,
Mr. Pulitzer prints your name
and how much you gave in his paper.

I am sending my two pet roosters.
Mr. Pulitzer can sell them and
use the money for the pedestal.
I can't wait to see my name in print.

People as far away as Texas have sent money —
soldiers, factory workers, miners, bank tellers,
actors, doctors, farmers, shopkeepers.
Even gamblers have given money.
The most money has come from
veterans of the Civil War.
They gave fifteen hundred dollars.

Two boys sent a dollar that
they had saved for circus tickets.
Another boy sent twenty-five pennies.

Mr. Pulitzer pokes fun
at the rich people who don't give.
He calls them "croakers" and "laggards"
and prints their names in his paper, too!

JOSEPH PULITZER
Publisher, New York *World*
New York City, August 1886

Liberty's skeleton is now anchored
to the pedestal,
bolted to huge girders
that protrude from the concrete.
Eighty-nine feet tall, twenty feet thick,
and faced with granite,
the pedestal is more majestic than I had hoped.
I am humbled by my readers' generosity.
Many who have so little gave so much
to build this noble structure.

Liberty arrived in 214 crates.
On her trip across the ocean,
vicious storms buffeted the ship.
Labels fell off crates.
Pieces of her copper skin were shaken.
Many need to be reshaped.

Slowly each copper sheet
is hoisted up with heavy ropes.
The workers sit on the crossbars,
fitting her copper skin to the skeleton.
When one piece doesn't fit,
they haul up another and try it,
then another,
until they find the right one.
The first piece of copper skin attached
to the skeleton is named "Bartholdi."
The second piece is christened "Pulitzer."

Each day she grows more beautiful.
I predict that those who once mocked her
will soon love her and understand
her power and significance.

JOSÉ MARTÍ
Journalist, Poet
New York City, October 28, 1886

Today is Liberty's day.
Up and down the Hudson River,
French and American flags stretch
from mast to mast, from bow to stern,
on hundreds of tugboats and yachts and
scows and steamers and ships-of-war.

Rain is falling, but no one cares.
The red, white, and blue of the Stars and Stripes
and the French tricolors fly
from buildings and stores and arches.
Sidewalks, doorways, windowsills, and roofs
bulge with people.
Adults stand on wooden boxes and scaffolding.
A million Americans have come to welcome her.

Grand Marshal Charles Stone,
astride a black horse, leads
five miles of red, gray, blue, and green.
Regiment after regiment.
Soldiers and sailors, young and old,
march in lockstep.
Eyes front, chests out, arms swinging.
Left, right, left, right.
Legs strut and splash themselves.

The militias dip their colors in tribute
at Pulitzer's building and the viewing stand.
The Rochambeau grenadiers raise
their glistening swords to their lips.
President Grover Cleveland salutes
the bullet-torn flags of past wars.
"Bartholdi! Bartholdi!" people cry
as they see him on the viewing stand.
Three girls race up to give him flowers.

Children in school uniforms,
heavy-footed policemen with shiny brass buttons,
firemen decked out in red shirts
alongside their horse-drawn steam engines,
cheering, "Hi-yi-yi-hi."
Navy men with big white hats.
Zouaves with fire-red pants.
Soldiers wounded in past wars ride
in carriages with judges and governors.

And the marching bands,
so many, all playing at once.
O say can you see . . .
Arise, ye sons of France, to glory . . .
I wish I was in the land of cotton . . .
I'm a Yankee Doodle Dandy . . .
A din of drums and horns and tubas.

Finally, General Washington's carriage,
drawn by eight dappled gray horses.
Yays and hoorays for the Continental Guards.
The city is one vast cheer.

Liberty! The most important word in the world.
I know that all too well.
I was deported from my country, Cuba,
for fighting to free my people from Spanish rule.

AUGUSTE BARTHOLDI
Sculptor
Bedloe's Island, October 28, 1886

Liberty's face is hidden beneath our tricolors.
I see easily through to her magnificence.

I wend my way through the crowd
to climb up to Liberty's crown.
Surrounded by her beams and ribs,
I mount the 354 steps, remembering
the hundreds of thousands of people —
French and American —
who helped realize my dream.
If only Laboulaye were alive to see her.

I crouch to look through her windows.
I wave to the boy below who will signal me
at just the right moment.
Tugboat whistles and trumpet fanfares
clash in the damp air.
Cannons fire deafening salutes.

Finally quiet. A blessing.
One speech. A second speech.
I cannot hear anything over
the shrieking tugboats.

The boy waves his hand.
At last, it is time.
I loosen the cord holding the tricolors
over Liberty's face.

The flag falls.
Lady Liberty is visible in all her glory.
Cheering and shouting rip the air.
Roaring cannons, belching foghorns,
drumrolls, trumpet flourishes.
Arise, ye sons of France, to glory . . .
O say can you see . . .

Every part of her shouts freedom.
In one hand she holds a tablet,
engraved with July 4, 1776.
In her other hand she holds a torch.
These flames do not destroy.
Mon Américaine does not conquer with weapons.
True liberty triumphs through Truth and Justice and Law.

She wears a flowing robe
like the ancient goddess *Libertas.*
Her right foot is raised.
Liberty walks.
Freedom never stands still.
A broken shackle and chain lie near her feet.
America broke the links of slavery
to fulfill its promise of equality for all.

President Cleveland steps forward.
The crowd quiets.
"We will not forget that Liberty
has made her home here," he says.

More cheering and shouting.
On and on, a glorious explosion of noise.
Like a hundred Bastille Day celebrations.

I feel perfect happiness.
This symbol of unity and friendship
between two great republics will last forever.
It has taken more than twenty years, but
the dream of my life is accomplished.

♦ ♦ ♦

DOREEN RAPPAPORT
New York City, Today

My grandfather left no written record of how he felt
when he first saw the Statue of Liberty. But many other
Americans have.

*You, American born, can never imagine how we, who
lived under all kinds of "isms," felt when we, in the early
hours of a very cold January morning, saw you, the
Statue of Liberty. To us, you meant real freedom.*

– Stelio M. Stelson,
from Turkey, September 1922

*I was wondering as I looked at you, "What is going to
happen to me in this vast new land of America?" But you
gave me courage . . . with the torch in your hand pointing
heavenward, and telling me as you have told millions of
others, "You are welcome to this new land."*

– Olaf Holen,
from Norway, May 1909

*I looked at that statue with a sense of
bewilderment, half doubting its reality. . . .
This symbol of America — this enormous
expression of what we had all been taught
was the inner meaning of this country we
were coming to — inspired awe.*

– Edward Corsi,
from Italy, 1907

*That's all my father ever talked about:
"When you see the Lady." He and his Lady.
My mother used to say, even in the last few
years, "Your father and his Lady."*

– Millie Kate Olthoff de Nigri,
from Germany, 1924

·STATUE OF LIBERTY DIMENSIONS·

HEIGHT FROM BASE TO TORCH: 151' 1"

HEIGHT FROM FOUNDATION TO TORCH: 305' 1"

HEIGHT FROM HEEL TO TOP OF HEAD: 111' 1"

LENGTH OF HAND: 16' 5"

LENGTH OF INDEX FINGER: 8' 0"

WIDTH OF HEAD FROM EAR TO EAR: 10' 0"

DISTANCE ACROSS EYE: 2' 6"

LENGTH OF NOSE: 4' 6"

LENGTH OF RIGHT ARM: 42' 0"

WIDTH OF RIGHT ARM AT GREATEST THICKNESS: 12' 0"

WIDTH OF MOUTH: 3' 0"

LENGTH OF TABLET: 23' 7"

WIDTH OF TABLET: 13' 7"

THICKNESS OF TABLET: 2' 0"

LENGTH OF TORCH: 21' 0"

HEIGHT OF GRANITE PEDESTAL: 89' 0"

HEIGHT OF CONCRETE FOUNDATION: 65' 0"

WEIGHT OF COPPER USED IN STATUE:
200,000 POUNDS (100 TONS)

WEIGHT OF STEEL USED IN STATUE:
250,000 POUNDS (125 TONS)

TOTAL WEIGHT OF STATUE:
450,000 POUNDS (225 TONS)

· IMPORTANT EVENTS ·

SUMMER 1865	◆ ◆ ◆	F. Auguste Bartholdi dines at Édouard-René Lefebvre de Laboulaye's home.
JUNE 8–OCTOBER 1871	◆ ◆ ◆	On a visit with Marie Simon to the U.S., Bartholdi selects Bedloe's Island as the site.
APRIL 1875	◆ ◆ ◆	The *Union Franco-Américaine* is founded with Laboulaye as the head. Fund-raising begins in France.
OCTOBER 26, 1875	◆ ◆ ◆	Laboulaye presents a formal request for Bedloe's Island to President Ulysses S. Grant.
NOVEMBER 1875	◆ ◆ ◆	The manufacturing of Liberty begins in Paris.
AUGUST 1876	◆ ◆ ◆	Liberty's arm and torch are exhibited at the Philadelphia Centennial Exhibition, and then in New York City.
FEBRUARY 1877	◆ ◆ ◆	Congress agrees to provide the site and money for her maintenance.
MARCH 1877	◆ ◆ ◆	An American fund-raising committee is formed.
OCTOBER 1877	◆ ◆ ◆	President Grant visits the workshop in Paris.
JUNE 1879–JULY 1880	◆ ◆ ◆	More than 250,000 francs is raised in France.
1879–1881	◆ ◆ ◆	A. Gustave Eiffel designs and supervises the statue's internal framework.
MARCH 1883	◆ ◆ ◆	Congress rejects a $100,000 request for pedestal construction.
MAY 25, 1883	◆ ◆ ◆	Édouard de Laboulaye dies.
JUNE 1883	◆ ◆ ◆	Joseph Pulitzer launches his first fund-raising campaign.
OCTOBER 1883–MAY 1884	◆ ◆ ◆	The foundation is built.
NOVEMBER 1883	◆ ◆ ◆	Emma Lazarus writes "The New Colossus."
JULY 4, 1884	◆ ◆ ◆	France formally gives the completed Statue of Liberty to the U.S.
AUGUST 7, 1884	◆ ◆ ◆	Richard Morris Hunt's design for the pedestal is accepted.
MARCH 16, 1885	◆ ◆ ◆	Joseph Pulitzer launches a second fund-raising campaign.
JUNE 1885	◆ ◆ ◆	The statue arrives in New York.
AUGUST 1885	◆ ◆ ◆	Joseph Pulitzer's newspaper raises $102,006.39 from 121,000 people.
NOVEMBER 1885	◆ ◆ ◆	Bartholdi spends three weeks in New York helping with the foundation.
APRIL 22, 1886	◆ ◆ ◆	Construction on the pedestal is finished.
AUGUST 4, 1886	◆ ◆ ◆	Congress approves $456,500 for the statue.
OCTOBER 28, 1886	◆ ◆ ◆	"Liberty Enlightening the World" is dedicated.
MAY 6, 1903	◆ ◆ ◆	"The New Colossus" is inscribed on a bronze plaque and mounted inside the pedestal.
OCTOBER 15, 1956	◆ ◆ ◆	The Statue of Liberty is proclaimed a national monument; Congress renames Bedloe's Island "Liberty Island."
1980–1986	◆ ◆ ◆	A major restoration for the statue's one-hundredth birthday is completed.

· AUTHOR'S NOTE ·

Many years ago a friend — a Hungarian Jew whose family had escaped from being deported to a Nazi concentration camp where millions of Jews were murdered — told me about the moment, in 1950, when her ship pulled into New York City's harbor. My eyes filled with tears as she described people running up to the deck from all parts of the ship, shouting, "The Lady! The Lady!" when they saw the Statue of Liberty for the very first time. Since then I have read numerous accounts by other immigrants describing similar joy at seeing this symbol of hope and freedom, and my eyes still fill with tears.

While researching the "biography" of the Statue of Liberty, I was struck by how many different people worked to make the statue a reality. The process was a long, hard struggle of twenty years. In first-person accounts, letters, newspaper articles, and books, Laboulaye, Bartholdi, Pulitzer, Eiffel, Lazarus, and Martí gave many details of their impressions, feelings, passion, and/or involvement in the story of how she came to be. I was amazed to learn that more than two hundred thousand French and American citizens had contributed money to build her. I searched and searched through the New York *World* until I found a letter written by a ten-year-old girl, Florence de Foreest. Her commitment to Liberty had inspired her to send her pet roosters to Joseph Pulitzer with instructions to sell them to raise money. After reading these accounts, I felt as if I knew these people. I decided that they should tell the life story of the Statue of Liberty. Their comments, experiences, and feelings are woven into my text.

I thank Julie Koven, reference librarian at the Jewish Historical Society, and Janet Levine, oral historian at the Ellis Island Immigration Museum. Barry Moreno, historian and librarian at the Statue of Liberty National Monument and Ellis Island, clarified all kinds of important information and read the manuscript for accuracy. I am grateful to my illustrator, Matt Tavares, for his exceptional commitment to detail, along with his striking artistic conception.

— Doreen Rappaport

· ILLUSTRATOR'S NOTE ·

When I first read Doreen Rappaport's manuscript, I was fascinated by the step-by-step process of how Lady Liberty grew from a four-foot clay model in Bartholdi's Paris studio into an enormous 151-foot copper colossus atop an 89-foot granite pedestal in New York Harbor. I was, and still am, amazed at the craftsmanship, skill, and collaboration involved in creating such a gigantic statue.

But this is not just a story about how a famous statue was built. Rather, it is a story about people. This story is told from several different points of view, and the characters all share a common bond: to them, liberty was not some abstract concept. America had just made it through the Civil War. Slavery had just recently been abolished. France was ruled by an emperor. They knew what it was like to live without liberty. To them, liberty was very real, and it was something worth fighting for and something worth celebrating.

When I painted the picture of the immigrant workers digging the hole for Liberty's foundation, I thought of my own grandfather, Manuel Tavares. He left his home in Portugal to come to America in 1918, when he was sixteen years old. There were no jobs in Portugal, and my grandfather was happy to find work operating a swing saw at a casket company in Cambridge, Massachusetts. Like the men who dug Liberty's foundation, he worked long hours, and I'm sure his muscles strained and his body ached. But he was grateful, because he was building a better life for himself and his family.

Before I started working on this book, I had never thought much about the Statue of Liberty. I thank Doreen Rappaport for opening my eyes to this remarkable part of our history. I would also like to thank Kristen Nobles, Mary Lee Donovan, Chris Paul, and Rosemary Stimola; and a special thanks to my family, for their love and support.

— Matt Tavares

· SELECTED SOURCES ·

American Committee of the Statue of Liberty. American Committee of the Statue of Liberty correspondence, 1881–1901. (This collection consists chiefly of letters by Bartholdi.)

Bartholdi, Frédéric Auguste. Frédéric Auguste Bartholdi papers, 1871. (Journal of Bartholdi's 1871 trip to the U.S. and letters to his mother during that journey.)

Blanchet, Christian. Translation by Bernard A. Weisberger. *Statue of Liberty: The First Hundred Years.* New York: American Heritage Press, 1985. Distributed by Houghton Mifflin.

Brownstone, David M., Irene M. Franck, and Douglass L. Brownstone. *Island of Hope, Island of Tears.* New York: Penguin, 1986.

Burchard, S. H. *The Statue of Liberty: Birth to Rebirth.* San Diego: Harcourt Brace Jovanovich, 1985.

Burns, Ken. *The Statue of Liberty.* [Video recording.] Alexandria, VA: PBS Home Video, 1996.

Dillon, Wilton. S, and Neil G. Kotler, eds. *The Statue of Liberty Revisited: Making a Universal Symbol.* Washington, DC: Smithsonian Institution Press, 1994.

Gray, Walter D. *Interpreting American Democracy in France: The Career of Édouard Laboulaye, 1811–1883.* London: Associated University Press, 1994.

Gschaedler, Andre. *True Light on the Statue of Liberty and Its Creator.* Narberth, PA: Livingston Publishing Company, 1966.

Moreno, Barry. *The Statue of Liberty Encyclopedia.* New York: Simon & Schuster, 2000.

Pauli, Hertha, and E. B. Ashton [pseud.]. *I Lift My Lamp: The Way of a Symbol.* New York: Appleton-Century-Crofts, 1948.

Schor, Esther. *Emma Lazarus.* New York: Nextbook/Schocken, 2006.

Statue of Liberty National Monument Historical Research House Study. *Construction History: The Statue, Its Pedestal and Foundation,* Books 1–3.

Vogel, Dan. *Emma Lazarus.* Boston: Twayne Publishers, 1980.

Young, Bette Roth. *Emma Lazarus in Her World: Life and Letters.* Philadelphia: Jewish Publication Society, 1995.

If you want to learn more about the Statue of Liberty, read:

Bunting, Eve. *A Picnic in October.* Illustrated by Nancy Carpenter. New York: Harcourt Brace & Company, 2004.

Curlee, Lynn. *Liberty.* New York: Simon & Schuster, 2000.

Drummond, Allan. *Liberty.* New York: Farrar, Straus & Giroux, 2002.

Hochain, Serge. *Building Liberty: A Statue Is Born.* Washington, DC: National Geographic Society, 2004.

Landau, Elaine. *The Statue of Liberty.* New York: Scholastic Library Publishing, 2004.

Maestro, Betsy. *The Story of the Statue of Liberty.* Illustrated by Guilio Maestro. New York: William Morrow, 1989.

Stevenson, Harvey. *Looking at Liberty.* New York: HarperCollins, 2003.

You can also visit the official website of the Statue of Liberty at www.nps.gov/stli

· INDEX ·

· INDEX CONTINUED ·

DOREEN RAPPAPORT is the author of many award-winning books for young readers, including a trilogy on the history of African Americans — *No More! Stories and Songs of Slave Resistance, Free at Last! Stories and Songs of Emancipation*, and *Nobody Gonna Turn Me 'Round: Stories and Songs of the Civil Rights Movement* — and *Beyond Courage: The Untold Story of Jewish Resistance During the Holocaust*. About *Lady Liberty*, she says, "Intertwined with the dream of a statue was the dream of America, the land of possibility. I wanted to show readers how the statue personified for so many the enviable concepts of freedom and self-government." Doreen Rappaport lives in Copake Falls, New York.

MATT TAVARES is the author-illustrator of *There Goes Ted Williams, Becoming Babe Ruth*, and *Henry Aaron's Dream*, and of *Zachary's Ball, Oliver's Game*, and *Mudball*. He has illustrated many other picture books besides. About *Lady Liberty*, he says, "What I loved most about this book was how personal it all felt. I tried to learn as much as I could about all those involved and did my best to show their intensity and capture their passion in my illustrations." Matt Tavares lives in Ogunquit, Maine.